Versatile Verbiage

Words take flight, like birds in the sky,
Dancing on pages where thoughts can fly.
Colors of language paint vivid scenes,
Whispers of stories tucked in between.

Verses like rivers, they twist and turn,
Flowing with meaning, eager to learn.
Sculpting emotions, they shape our minds,
In every heartbeat, true art finds.

From sonnets to limericks, styles collide,
Crafting a symphony, joy cannot hide.
Echoes of laughter, the pain of goodbye,
Each word a vessel, we reach for the sky.

In silence, they linger, in chaos, they soar,
Armies of verbiage at every door.
Open the pages, let stories ignite,
Versatile words, your guiding light.

Fragments and Form

In broken pieces, beauty lies,
Shattered dreams in painted skies.
Each fragment holds a story clear,
Whispers echo, drawing near.

Shapes of sorrow, joy entwined,
In the chaos, we must find.
A mosaic of the heart's own beat,
Crafted tales where life is sweet.

Word Artistry

Brush of language, stroke of heart,
Every word a work of art.
Colors dance in rhythm true,
Painting visions old and new.

Whispers weave through silent air,
Stories linger everywhere.
Crafting meaning, bold and bright,
Words ignite the inner light.

The Grid of Grief

In the patterns, pain aligns,
Lines of loss, where sorrow binds.
Each square marks a silent tear,
Holding memories held so dear.

Through the maze, the heart will roam,
Finding solace, finding home.
In the grid, both dark and light,
Grief transforms into the night.

Printed Pathways

On pages worn, our footsteps trace,
Stories etched in time and space.
Paths of ink, in rows they flow,
Guiding us where dreams shall go.

Each chapter brings a new embrace,
Familiar faces, a warm grace.
In printed words, we find the way,
Light the path for a brighter day.

Shadows of Syntax

In whispers of dusk, the letters align,
Crafting meanings, both fragile and fine.
Each phrase a brushstroke, painting the night,
In shadows of syntax, where dreams take flight.

The grammar of silence, a language unspun,
Echoes of thoughts, like whispers they run.
Capturing moments, fleeting and bright,
In shadows of syntax, obscured from sight.

The Geometry of Emotion

Angles of heartbeats, a measure of pain,
Circles of laughter, like sun after rain.
Triangles form in the gaze we exchange,
The geometry of emotion, beautifully strange.

Lines of connection, drawn in the air,
Shapes of our stories, a bond we both share.
With curves of compassion, we find our way,
The geometry of emotion, in light of the day.

Formed by Words

In silence we gather, our thoughts intertwined,
A tapestry woven, each thread defined.
Stories are born, from whispers and sighs,
Formed by words, under vast, open skies.

From pages of history, to futures unclear,
The voices of poets are always so near.
Each syllable dances, each verse a refrain,
Formed by words, like sweet summer rain.

Stanzas in Structure

A rhythm of thoughts, in verses confined,
Stanzas in structure, where echoes unwind.
Each line a heartbeat, a pulse in the night,
In poetry's dance, we find our insight.

Bound by the meter, yet soaring so free,
The beauty of language, a river at sea.
With each carefully placed, like bricks in a wall,
Stanzas in structure, we rise, we fall.

Enigmatic Structures

In shadows deep, figures play,
Twisting paths, lead us astray.
Whispers call from heights unknown,
Silhouettes of dreams we've sown.

Echoed thoughts in silent halls,
Mysteries wrapped in ancient walls.
Each turn reveals the unseen line,
A puzzle knit by design.

Written Geometries

Angles sharp, the words align,
Constructing thoughts, a grand design.
Lines converge in perfect grace,
Shapes that form a timeless space.

Circles hold reflections bright,
In every turn, a spark of light.
Patterns rise from ink-stained hands,
Drafting dreams in shifting sands.

Inked Visions

Brush of ink on paper wide,
Capturing visions that bide.
Figures dance in fluid streams,
As color flows through whispered dreams.

The canvas breathes, alive with thought,
A tapestry of battles fought.
With each stroke, a world awakes,
A vivid dream that never shakes.

Poetry as Concrete

Sturdy verses, firm and bold,
Solid stories, truths retold.
Chiseled lines that pierce the air,
Each word a block, built with care.

Foundations laid of spoken art,
In every slab, a beating heart.
From rough edges, beauty grows,
A structure where the spirit glows.

Word-Warped Spaces

In corners of the mind, they dance,
Unraveled thoughts in a fleeting glance.
Colors clash and shapes collide,
In this realm where dreams reside.

Words twist and turn, a playful kite,
Soaring high, out of sheer delight.
Fractured phrases, a vibrant maze,
Lost in this word-warped haze.

Echoes in Edges

Whispers linger on the edge of night,
Softly woven in fading light.
Fragments echo in shadows cast,
Time unfurls, a fleeting past.

Between the lines, a silent song,
Resonates where we belong.
In every pause, a heartbeat calls,
Echoes linger, where silence falls.

Bridging Words

Across the gap, we stretch and reach,
In stories shared, we find our speech.
Connecting souls, a tender thread,
In whispered hopes, our hearts are fed.

Each syllable a stepping stone,
Building bridges, not alone.
In every tale, a world unfolds,
With love and truth in words of gold.

The Fabric of Expression

Stitches woven through time and space,
Crafting stories that interlace.
Colors of feeling, textures of thought,
In every seam, a lesson taught.

Threads of laughter, strands of tears,
Embroidered hopes throughout the years.
Together we create, hand in hand,
A tapestry that will ever stand.

The Geometry of Language

Words form shapes within our minds,
Angles sharp, where meaning binds.
Curve of thought, a gentle bend,
In every line, new worlds extend.

Letters dance in structured grace,
A matrix built, an endless space.
Connections made through silent sound,
In this blueprint, we are found.

Stanzas in Stone

Carved with care on ancient walls,
Whispers echo, memory calls.
Each stanza stands a tale to tell,
In hardened rock, dreams dwell.

Mossy verses, time's embrace,
Nature's ink, a sacred place.
Through seasons passed, they still endure,
A testament, a vision pure.

Arranged Echoes

Voices blend in rhythmic play,
Harmonies chased, then drift away.
In every note, a story waits,
Resonating through time's gates.

Echoes linger, soft and clear,
Past and present drawing near.
In careful lines, their pulse resides,
A symphony where truth abides.

Typography's Dance

Fonts collide in vibrant hues,
Letters sway, a lively muse.
Curves and lines in dynamic form,
Creating warmth, a gentle norm.

In every page, a rhythm flows,
As chaos tames and beauty grows.
Typography, with flair and chance,
Invites the words to take a dance.

Carved Scribbles

In the bark, tales lie still,
Whispers of wind, dreams to fulfill.
Roots entwined in secrets deep,
Nature's cryptic notes, hers to keep.

Lines of life, twisted, turned,
In shadows cast, a fire burned.
Embers of thoughts upon the tree,
Carved in silence, wild and free.

Shapes of Whimsy

Balloons afloat in summer skies,
Clouds like castles, with playful cries.
Butterflies dance on petals bright,
Colors mingling in pure delight.

Dreams are painted in swirls and twirls,
A canvas where laughter unfurls.
In the breeze, a giggle grows,
Whimsy sown wherever it goes.

Messages in Mosaics

Pieces scattered, stories unfold,
Crafted in fragments, treasures of gold.
Each tile a whisper, a voice from the past,
Gathered in beauty, forever to last.

A puzzle of colors, a tale intertwined,
In every shard, a world defined.
Artful glimpses of moments we share,
Mosaics of love, sewn with care.

Hidden Harmonies

In the rustle of leaves, a soft song plays,
Nature's chorus in radiant rays.
A heartbeat thrums in the quiet night,
Whispers of stars, pure and bright.

Melodies weave through the fabric of time,
Silent symphonies in rhythm and rhyme.
Echoes of dreams in the stillness we find,
Harmonies linger, forever entwined.

Design of Diction

Words weave together,
Painting thoughts so bright,
A tapestry of meaning,
In day and in night.

Each phrase finds its place,
Crafted with pure care,
A melody of voices,
Harmonies laid bare.

In whispers and echoes,
They dance with delight,
Choosing just the right tone,
To fill hearts with light.

The power of language,
A treasure to behold,
Unlocking hidden stories,
In letters bold.

Structure in Verses

Lines stand like soldiers,
Uniform and strong,
Each holds its own purpose,
In the poet's song.

Rhythms create patterns,
Weaving through the page,
A dance of expression,
That never grows age.

Stanzas form a fortress,
Guarding precious words,
While meter flows freely,
Like songs of the birds.

With discipline and grace,
Verses take their flight,
Crafting worlds from silence,
In the dark of night.

Shape-Shifting Narratives

Stories twist and turn,
Like paths in a maze,
Unfolding their secrets,
In mysterious ways.

Characters emerge,
In shadows and light,
Transforming their fates,
In the depths of the night.

Plotlines break the mold,
And leap through the air,
Turning hopes into dreams,
Surpassing despair.

With every page turned,
A new truth is found,
Shape-shifting narratives,
In silence resound.

The Art of Arrangement

Fragments of a thought,
Placed just so with care,
A balance of chaos,
And order that's rare.

Chorus and refrain,
In a delicate dance,
Echoes of feelings,
That spark the romance.

Each element chosen,
To create a whole,
A symphony of ideas,
That feed the soul.

In this crafted space,
Ideas take their stance,
The art of arrangement,
Gives meaning a chance.

Dances of Design

In twilight's glow, colors entwine,
Shapes sway gently, in perfect line.
A canvas breathes, with whispers bold,
Each stroke a tale, a dream retold.

Patterns rise, like waves of the sea,
Crafted with care, in harmony.
Fingers trace paths, both soft and sharp,
Creating magic, a silent harp.

Geometry sings, in arcs and folds,
Elegance captured, in hues of gold.
Symmetry dances, a fleeting ghost,
In every design, we find our host.

The night unravels, with stars above,
In every twist, there's a hint of love.
Art blooms gently, in hearts refined,
Dances of design, forever entwined.

The Aesthetics of Words

Words weave lightly, like petals in spring,
Each letter a note, in songs we sing.
Their beauty captured, in stories spun,
A tapestry formed, as bright as the sun.

Metaphors blossom, rich with delight,
Painting our thoughts in the softest light.
Rhymes tether dreams, like stars in the sky,
Launching our voices, allowing us to fly.

In silence, we listen, to verses unseen,
The echoes of wisdom, in spaces between.
Punctuation sways, like dancers in time,
Creating a rhythm, pure and sublime.

In every chapter, new worlds ignite,
The aesthetics of words, a luminous sight.
Crafting connections, hearts unconfined,
In the realm of language, we are aligned.

Ink and Stone

Ink flows freely, a river of thought,
Crafted on paper, where dreams are caught.
Each mark a journey, from mind to page,
Stories awakened, breaking the cage.

Stone stands solid, a guardian's keep,
Etched with whispers, of secrets deep.
Time cannot fade, the tales it holds,
In the heart of the mountains, history unfolds.

Together they dance, ink meets the rock,
In a timeless bond, they softly talk.
Textured and rich, the past comes alive,
In ink and stone, our spirits strive.

Through shadows and light, they forever blend,
A testament true, where beginnings mend.
Ink and stone sing, in unity's tone,
Creating a legacy, forever our own.

Whispering Lines

Whispering lines, trace the edge of dreams,
Curves and angles, like flowing streams.
They beckon softly, with secrets to share,
In the quiet of night, a delicate air.

Letters entwine, in dances so light,
Filling the voids, with stories of night.
Each loop and swirl, a heartbeat's song,
Inviting reflections, where we belong.

Bridges of thought, connect heart to hand,
Sketches of hope, in a vast, soft land.
Ink spills like rain, on the canvas of soul,
Framing the moments that make us whole.

The art of our lives, in every design,
Whispering lines, eternally shine.
Through shadows and colors, we bravely find,
The gentle embrace of the heart and mind.

Lines that Live

Words dance lightly in the air,
Whispers trace the thoughts we share.
Moments captured, never fade,
In the heart, their echoes laid.

Stories woven with each breath,
Life's brief canvas, art from death.
In shadows cast, in sunlight bright,
Our lines take form, a dance of light.

Visual Verses

Colors splash across the page,
Painting feelings with each sage.
Imagery that speaks so clear,
Visions bright that draw us near.

Shapes of love, of loss, of hope,
In each stroke, we learn to cope.
Art and words entwined as one,
A masterpiece when all is done.

Fragments of the Mind

Thoughts like shards of glass they gleam,
Reflecting light, revealing dreams.
Scattered pieces, puzzle whole,
In these fragments, find the soul.

Each memory, a fleeting glance,
A whispered truth, a secret dance.
In the chaos, beauty holds,
A tapestry of tales unfolds.

The Poetry Beneath

In silence lies the sweetest song,
A gentle hum where we belong.
In hidden depths, our voices rise,
The poetry beneath the skies.

Nature whispers in quiet tune,
Beneath the sun, beneath the moon.
A symphony of heart and breath,
Life's verses woven close to death.

Sculpted Sentences

Each word carves deep, profound,
In silence, thoughts are found.
Through shadows, light may creep,
In stories we have drowned.

Crafting lines with gentle grace,
Our dreams begin to trace.
A rhythm formed, a delicate lace,
In each heart, a sacred space.

Strokes of ink on empty page,
Capturing every age.
Whispered truths we engage,
On this literary stage.

The Form of Expression

In every twist, a tale resides,
Where meaning shifts and slides.
With every phrase, one confides,
In words, our spirit abides.

From depths of joy to shades of pain,
Emotions flow like rain.
Through every loss and every gain,
In lines, we break the chain.

Crafted thoughts like woven thread,
In every heart, they've bled.
The stories that we've read,
In silence, are still said.

Textual Landscapes

Across the page, horizons bloom,
In written worlds, dispel the gloom.
Mountains rise and valleys loom,
In every word, there's room.

Rivers of thought run deep and wide,
With currents strong, they glide.
In this realm, where dreams abide,
Imagination's our guide.

Fields of phrases stretch and sway,
In this landscape, we play.
With every dawn, a new array,
In words, we lose our way.

Bound by Letters

In every letter, bonds are formed,
Through ink and paper, souls are warmed.
With every story, hearts are stormed,
In silence, deep emotions swarmed.

Pages turn, and worlds collide,
In shadows long, where dreams reside.
With trust, we share what we can't hide,
In words, we find our guide.

Bound by tales both old and new,
In this dance, we find what's true.
Letters weave and break on cue,
In paragraphs, our spirits flew.

Patterns of Thought

In quiet corners of the mind,
Ideas swirl, entwined and twined.
Each thought a thread, a vibrant hue,
Weaving worlds both old and new.

Echoes dance in mental space,
Chasing shadows, finding grace.
A labyrinth of bright designs,
In every corner, wisdom shines.

Questions bloom like flowers rare,
Seeking truth in open air.
With every twist, a pathway grows,
In patterns where imagination flows.

So listen closely, hear the sounds,
Of inner worlds that know no bounds.
Patterns shift, as thoughts collide,
In the tapestry where dreams abide.

Verses in the Void

In silence, echoes softly call,
Craving meaning, feeling small.
Words suspended in the dark,
Flickering like a distant spark.

Thoughts adrift in empty space,
Searching for a warm embrace.
Verses linger, time stands still,
Becoming whispers, bending will.

Yet in this void, a truth unfolds,
Stories woven, mysteries told.
Emptiness can hold such weight,
With space to think, create, and wait.

So let the silence pave the way,
For verses born from night and day.
In every gap, a chance to find,
The poetry of heart and mind.

Layers of Meaning

Beneath the surface, layers lie,
Secrets hidden, truth awry.
Words like stones, tossed in a stream,
Ripple out, unraveling a dream.

Interpretations twist and bend,
Each layer leading to a friend.
A simple phrase can spark a flame,
In every heart, the quest the same.

Peeling back the skin of thought,
Revelations sought, wisdom caught.
In stories told, and tales retold,
Layers reveal what hearts behold.

Dive deep into the rich design,
Where meaning waits, both yours and mine.
Let every word, a seed, take flight,
In layers of day and velvet night.

The Architecture of Verse

Within the lines, a frame is found,
A structure built upon the ground.
Each stanza shapes a sturdy wall,
Rising up, refusing to fall.

Rhythms pulse like heartbeats sound,
Creating echoes all around.
The space between is just as key,
In haunting halls of memory.

Metaphors, like arches tall,
Hold up the weight of thoughts that sprawl.
Each word a brick, each rhyme a beam,
Constructing dreams, igniting theme.

So walk the paths of this design,
Where every verse seeks to align.
In the architecture's graceful dance,
A world awaits, a whispered chance.

Letters in Lockdown

In silence, words take flight,
Each pen stroke, a spark of light.
Pages whisper in the night,
Letters sealed, hearts in sight.

Dreams unfold, in ink they flow,
Sharing stories, to and fro.
Through the cracks, emotions show,
Locked away, yet we still grow.

Time stands still, as we write on,
Each phrase a thread, a woven dawn.
In solitude, our thoughts are drawn,
Communion found, through paper's song.

Love persists, though distanced far,
In every line, a guiding star.
Letters cast like nets from afar,
Binding us, where hearts ajar.

Tactile Tales

Fingers trace each line, a guide,
On textured pages, worlds collide.
Stories breathe, no need to hide,
In gentle touch, dreams reside.

Each curve of ink, a secret spun,
In every touch, the tale is won.
Feel the pulse of thoughts undone,
Tactile whispers, weaving fun.

The rough and smooth, they intertwine,
Emotions felt, like aged wine.
Every word, a road defined,
In tactile realms, our souls align.

Crafted tales where hands have danced,
Through sensing each, our hearts are chanced.
In moments shared, we've all advanced,
Tactile tales, where dreams romanced.

Sculpting Meaning

Chiseling thoughts from stones of grey,
Each word a shape, a bright array.
Sculpted minds, we carve the way,
In shadows cast, our truths will stay.

Fingers molded, bringing light,
Through frozen forms, we ignite.
Chiseled edges, sharp and bright,
Art unfolds in the dead of night.

Layers shed, revealing core,
In passion's heat, we seek to score.
Sculpting feelings, we explore,
Meaning finds us, forevermore.

Stone meets soul in gentle dance,
Finding purpose, a second chance.
In every curve, we take a stance,
Sculpting meaning, in life's expanse.

Text Weaving

Threads of language snugly spun,
Each word a stitch, our tales begun.
Looming visions, spun in fun,
Text weaving, where dreams are run.

Colors blend in patterns bright,
Emotions dance in woven light.
In every line, we find our plight,
Text weaving, a shared insight.

The fabric's strong, yet soft and free,
In every thread, our history.
Together, crafting tapestry,
Text weaving, a bond, you and me.

Through the warp, we bind and stitch,
Creating worlds, in every pitch.
In stories told, we find our niche,
Text weaving, our hearts enrich.

Semantic Silhouettes

In shadows of thought, meanings entwine,
Words dance lightly, secrets they confine.
Each phrase a whisper, a delicate trace,
Illuminating corners of time and space.

Echoes of language, softly they play,
Casting reflections in hues of gray.
Imagined forms that flicker and fade,
In the depth of silence, connections are made.

Through layers of context, we weave and we mold,
Crafting narratives, both new and old.
From letters to shapes, the stories emerge,
In the realm of thought, our dreams converge.

As shadows recede, clarity gleams,
Semantic silhouettes reveal hidden dreams.
With each revelation, a new path ignites,
Guiding us gently through shadowy nights.

Crafting with Language

With a sculptor's grace, we shape every term,
Molding the rhythm, letting thoughts squirm.
Every word chosen, a tool in our hand,
Crafting creations remarkably planned.

Layers of meaning in textures we find,
Patterns of stories, intricately lined.
A tapestry woven from heart and from mind,
In the art of our crafting, new worlds we bind.

Threads of connection in sentences bridge,
Words chosen wisely, never a grudge.
Through valleys of syntax, we journey along,
Expressing emotions in beat and in song.

In the workshop of language, we shape, we refine,
Finding the beauty in each little line.
From whispers to shouts, every voice in the fray,
Crafting with language, come what may.

Paved Imagination

On roads of our thoughts, imagination flows,
Paving the pathways where inspiration grows.
Each step a vision, each turn a surprise,
A journey through landscapes, where wonder lies.

Brick by brick, we lay down our dreams,
Constructing a realm where light brightly beams.
In the corners of mind, possibilities gleam,
Each idea a seed, each hope a bright beam.

With colors of creativity, the canvas unfolds,
Stories emerging, rich and bold.
In the gardens of thought, we nurture and tend,
Paved imagination, where horizons extend.

Through forests of fiction, we wander and roam,
Finding our place, building a home.
With each paved path, new adventures ignite,
In the landscape of dreams, everything feels right.

Visions in Varnish

With a glossy finish, dreams come alive,
Visions in varnish, where colors derive.
Layers of brightness, each stroke a delight,
Crafting the canvas, from morning to night.

In the sheen of the surface, reflections appear,
Moments and memories, precious and clear.
Every hue a story, every gloss a smile,
Painting our lives, going the extra mile.

Through the brush of our thoughts, creativity flows,
In visions of varnish, our artistry glows.
With polish and patience, we capture the grace,
Transforming the mundane into a dance of space.

As we step back, the masterpiece gleams,
In the heart of the art, we find our themes.
Visions in varnish, forever preserved,
In the gallery of hope, our passions served.

The Palette of Prose

Words like colors, bright and bold,
Crafting stories yet untold.
Emotions splash on empty page,
Artistry of every age.

Each sentence paints a vivid scene,
Layers rich in meaning's sheen.
With strokes of thought, we weave our thread,
In corridors of dreams we've tread.

Textures shift from soft to stark,
Illuminating shadows dark.
A brush of laughter, a dash of tear,
Each stroke beats softly near.

The canvas broad, the palette wide,
In prose we find our hearts reside.
With every word our colors blend,
A masterpiece that has no end.

Mosaics of Meaning

Fragments scatter, pieces roam,
Shards of thought that find a home.
Each tile tells a tale anew,
Crafted stories we pursue.

In patterns bright, through light and shade,
Crafting insights, never fade.
A tapestry woven in rich array,
Our voices rise, a grand display.

With every chip, a life unfolds,
In muted whispers, truths are told.
Mosaics dance in vibrant hues,
Inviting hearts, igniting views.

In every glance, a world to see,
Diverse perspectives, wild and free.
Together formed, a tale we share,
In unity, we breathe the air.

Language Landscapes

Words like rivers, flowing wide,
Carving valleys, deep inside.
Mountains rise with every verse,
In landscapes vast, we both converse.

Fields of thought and forests deep,
In whispers soft, our secrets keep.
The sky above, a canvas bright,
With clouds of dreams that take to flight.

Paths unworn, adventures call,
In language spaces, we stand tall.
Together traversing hill and glade,
In every heartbeat, magic laid.

From horizon's edge to ocean's shore,
In this vast world, we seek for more.
With every word, new lands appear,
In language journeys, hearts draw near.

The Solid State of Verse

In stanzas formed, we find our ground,
With rhythms locked in silent sound.
Each line, a pillar, strong and true,
In built foundations, thoughts renewed.

Verses stand like bricks in place,
Creating walls that time will trace.
In solid state, our words unite,
A fortress built in day and night.

Emotion echoes through the stone,
In every line, a heart is known.
With rhymes that bind and truths that flow,
A testament to all we know.

Through crafted verse, we reach the skies,
With every stanza, hope will rise.
In solid state, we find our voice,
In written worlds, we make our choice.

Whispers in the Subtext

In shadows deep, the stories lie,
Soft echoes brush the mind's eye.
Hidden truths in silence dwell,
A whispered truth, a softly told spell.

Beneath the surface, meanings dance,
A fleeting thought, a fleeting glance.
In muted tones, the heart can hear,
The quiet sighs that draw us near.

Between the lines, a world unfolds,
In gentle whispers, secrets hold.
Each fleeting breath, a tale we weave,
In whispered tones, we learn to believe.

In every pause, the stories grow,
In hushed confessions, we come to know.
So listen close, as silence sings,
The layers deep, the truth it brings.

Cadences Cast in Cement

In urban streets, the rhythm plays,
Concrete beats in myriad ways.
With every step, a tale is spun,
Each echo marks what we have done.

The city breathes in silent hum,
While dreams abound in the beats that come.
Streets where footsteps lay their claim,
A concrete dance, a living frame.

Brick by brick, the stories rise,
In steel and stone, the heart complies.
A cadence carved in weathered grace,
In every corner, a timeless trace.

Resonant tunes beneath the sun,
In every crack, a song begun.
With every note, the day we mend,
In cemented dreams, the past transcend.

The Structure of Sound

In vibrant waves, the music flows,
Creating worlds, where silence goes.
From whispered notes to thunderous bass,
Each sound builds a unique space.

Harmony breathes among the strings,
Melodies soar, as the heart sings.
Frequency paints the air with light,
A journey spun from day to night.

In every echo, truths collide,
With rhythms strong, we coincide.
Resonance, the language we share,
In every note, we find our care.

So let the sound structure our day,
In every heartbeat, come what may.
The world alive in tones profound,
Together, we dance, the structure of sound.

Expressions Embedded

In every gaze, a story told,
In fleeting moments, emotions bold.
Expressions carved on faces spread,
A language formed by words unsaid.

With every smile, a spark ignites,
In laughter shared, the darkness bites.
In sighs and frowns, we find our way,
Through silent tales of day to day.

Intricate layers within a glance,
In subtle gestures, hearts advance.
From autumn leaves to summer skies,
Expressions echo, never disguise.

So let us wear our truths with pride,
In every moment, let love guide.
In whispered expressions, we become,
A tapestry where all are one.

The Shape of Silence

In quiet corners, shadows play,
The whispers dance, then fade away.
Thoughts crystallize in muted tones,
As echoes linger, hearts atone.

Time stretches thin, a fragile thread,
Between the words that go unsaid.
Stillness wraps the world so tight,
A silent song that knows no light.

Beneath the calm, a storm may rise,
Unspoken truths in hidden skies.
The shape of silence, vast and wide,
Holds secrets deep, where dreams abide.

In every pause, a story waits,
Within the hush, creation sates.
So listen close, let silence speak,
And in its depths, find what you seek.

Vertices of Thought

At the edge of reason, ideas collide,
Sharp angles meet where doubts reside.
In the labyrinth of the mind,
Vertices of thought we seek to find.

Connections form in tangled lines,
As insights grow, like ancient vines.
Each twist and turn reveals the light,
In shadows cast by day and night.

Out here alone, the thoughts expand,
Daring to reach for the unplanned.
In every corner, questions bloom,
Vertices of thought dispel the gloom.

So forge ahead through paths unknown,
Where whispered dreams can be overthrown.
Each vertex holds a key to free,
The maze of thoughts, our destiny.

Echoes in the Margins

In faded pages, echoes dwell,
Whispers of stories, hard to tell.
Notes in the margins, sketched in haste,
Traces of thoughts that time won't waste.

Flickering memories brush the page,
Lost in the rush of a silent stage.
Each scribbled line, a secret kept,
A testament to the dreams we've wept.

In quiet corners, they softly resonate,
Filling the void, as voices wait.
Unwritten chapters, longing to start,
Echoes in the margins touch the heart.

So turn the page, let echoes rise,
In these whispers, find the ties.
For every note in shadows cast,
In margins found, our truths hold fast.

Sculpted Verses

With careful hands, the words take form,
Rising like figures in a storm.
Each line a chisel, each rhyme a stone,
Sculpted verses, etched alone.

In the chaos, artistry unfolds,
Narratives shaped like tales of old.
The heart of poetry, bare and bright,
Crafts sculptures borne from day and night.

Every stanza, a polished grace,
Chiseled deep in time and space.
From thoughts that linger, dreams arise,
Sculpted verses become the skies.

So let your words take flight and soar,
In every sculpted verse, explore.
Through ink and page, let stories mold,
And carve your truth, a tale retold.

Ink and Form

In the shadow of the page,
Ink flows like whispered dreams,
Capturing thoughts in a cage,
Crafting lives into seams.

Shapes emerge from the dark,
Curved lines dance in the night,
Each stroke leaves a mark,
Filling silence with light.

Stories hide in the blend,
Fates entwined in the scroll,
Pages twist, bend, and mend,
Ink unveils the soul's toll.

In the depths, we transform,
Words breathe life into lore,
Ink and paper perform,
In a world we explore.

Shapes of Silence

In a room devoid of sound,
Shadows whisper their form,
Shapes of silence abound,
In the stillness, they swarm.

Echoes flicker and fade,
Glimmers lost to the air,
Crafted moments displayed,
In the void, we all stare.

Silent tales intertwine,
Bound by thoughts yet unspun,
Hidden truths softly shine,
In the dark, they're not done.

Silence speaks in the night,
Forms dance in quiet grace,
In shadows, we find light,
A shape in empty space.

Words in the Walls

Behind the plaster and stone,
Whispers cling to the seams,
Words etched deep, overthrown,
In the quiet, they dream.

Echoes of laughter and pain,
Secrets carved with a knife,
Each word like a soft rain,
Washing the dust of life.

Time wraps stories in dust,
History lives in the cracks,
In the silence, we trust,
In the whispers, there's facts.

Listen close to the walls,
They hold truths, still and small,
In their silence, it calls,
For the past knows it all.

Letters Beneath the Surface

Beneath the tranquil tide,
Whispers of letters collide,
Messages from the deep,
In the ocean, they sleep.

Time-worn scripts echo clear,
Carried far by the waves,
Stories lost, yet they steer,
Into the hearts of the brave.

Secrets hidden from sight,
Wrapped in currents that flow,
Letters in the moonlight,
Cast a soft, gentle glow.

In the depths, they reside,
Waiting for souls to find,
Wisdom in every tide,
Letters lost, intertwined.

Lines of Expression

In shadows where silence sings,
A symphony of whispered things,
Each stroke of ink, a heart laid bare,
The rhythm of thoughts, light as air.

Words dance on pages, soft and free,
Painting the soul's quiet plea,
Emotions spill, a vivid stream,
Crafting the fabric of a dream.

Ink stains tell tales of joy and pain,
A canvas that thrives in sunshine and rain,
Every letter a step on the path,
Tracing the lines of an endless math.

These lines of expression, a timeless art,
A reflection, a story, a piece of the heart.

Tangible Dreams

In the realm where wishes reside,
A tapestry woven, side by side,
Each thread a hope, a longing sigh,
Reaching out toward the vast blue sky.

Concrete visions, bold and bright,
Stand firm against the fading night,
With every step on this sturdy ground,
Tangible dreams begin to abound.

In the cradle of dawn's soft glow,
Possibilities rise, like the tide's flow,
Every heartbeat echoes the scheme,
Awakening life from a fragile dream.

So, dare to grasp what seems so far,
For dreams are not just a flickering star,
With hands outstretched, we shall create,
A reality born from love, not fate.

Chiseled Rhyme

In stone-cold verses, hearts are chiseled,
With every word, our spirits twizzled,
Sculpting thoughts with a hammer's grace,
Beauty revealed in the time we face.

An artist's touch, with fervent might,
Carving shadows into the light,
Each syllable sharp, each beat refined,
A testament true of the heart and mind.

Verses echo like ancient halls,
Resonating through time's vast calls,
Layer by layer, we build our tale,
A harmonious structure that never grows stale.

So let us chisel, both bold and fine,
In the granite of life, we define,
With every rhyme, a part of the climb,
Creating our legacy, one word, one time.

The Architecture of Feeling

Within the framework, feelings rise,
Each emotion a room, a place to disguise,
From joy's bright sun to sorrow's dark night,
The architecture of feeling, a stunning sight.

Walls built of laughter, foundations of tears,
Echoes of whispers, the sum of our years,
In this vast structure, we learn to explore,
Each layer revealing insights and more.

Windows open wide to the world's embrace,
Inviting each moment, a kiss of grace,
In the corridors of time we roam,
Building a refuge, a place we call home.

So let us create, with love and with care,
A sanctuary molded in dreams we share,
For in the architecture of feeling we find,
The blueprint of life, beautifully aligned.

Inscriptions of Identity

In shadows cast by memories,
We find the stories of our souls.
Each line a mark, a whisper shared,
In the tapestry of our roles.

Names inscribed on stone and leaf,
Echoes of a history vast.
Fragments of a life now lived,
In hearts, the future and the past.

Through trials faced and bridges burned,
Each scar a badge of truth we wear.
In the fabric of our being,
Identity's essence laid bare.

The ink may fade, but will remain,
A testament to who we are.
In every choice, in love and pain,
The path we walk, our guiding star.

The Blueprint of Life

Lines and curves that intertwine,
Sketching paths in the vast unknown.
Each decision like a thread,
Woven into seeds we've sown.

With heartbeats tracing rhythms strong,
The craft of living takes its form.
In chaos and in calm, we find,
Designs that bend and shapes that warm.

Eras dance on paper trails,
Pages filled with dreams and fears.
Blueprints inked with hopes worn thin,
Fragile yet enduring years.

From silent nights to blazing days,
Life unfolds, a work of art.
Each moment etched in space and time,
An intricate map of the heart.

Language in Layers

Words climb and spiral, reaching high,
Each layer holds a meaning deep.
In silence, echoes of the past,
A lexicon of dreams we keep.

Voices rise in symphony,
Muffled notes of joy and pain.
Stripped back layers reveal truths,
In every heart, a lover's strain.

From whispered tales to shouts of love,
The tongue weaves beauty in the air.
Each syllable a brushstroke wide,
Painting emotions we all share.

In every culture, in every land,
The very essence of our kind.
Each layer built, a bridge of trust,
Connecting souls, though different minds.

Melodies in Material

In whispered winds and rustling leaves,
Nature sings a song so true.
Every stone and grain of sand,
Resonates in tones anew.

Crafted hands and minds collide,
Creating harmony in clay.
The rhythm flows through wood and steel,
In every touch, the heart will play.

From string to skin, a symphony,
Instruments embrace their fate.
The world hums to a quiet beat,
Melodies we cultivate.

In every heartbeat, every breath,
Resonance connects us all.
In tactile forms and sounds we weave,
Life's music, a universal call.

Tangibility of Emotion

In shadows deep, feelings dance,
They twist and turn, a fleeting chance.
With each heartbeat, colors blend,
A vivid story, we pen.

Whispers soft in the night air,
Fleeting moments, rich and rare.
Sadness drapes like velvet cloth,
Joy ignites like a sudden froth.

Memories linger, sweet and sour,
In every tear, in every hour.
Tear-streaked faces, laughter shared,
The weight of love, forever bared.

Fingers trace what hearts can't hold,
Emotions wild, both brave and bold.
In every touch, in every sigh,
The tangible bridge that won't deny.

The Dimension of Dreams

In twilight hues, where shadows play,
A world unfolds, in soft array.
Stars shimmer with whispers of light,
Guiding hearts through the velvet night.

Winds carry secrets of our hopes,
Through silent valleys, where magic gropes.
Each wish a ticket, each thought a flight,
To realms where the impossible feels right.

Awake or slumber, lines blur and bend,
In this domain, where dreams ascend.
With every heartbeat, a vision spins,
In woven tales, our journey begins.

Colorful canvases of what could be,
Each stroke of fate, a mystery.
In exploration, our spirits soar,
Dimensions vast, forevermore.

Crystallized Ideas

Glimmers flicker in the mind's eye,
Thoughts take shape, as moments fly.
Like crystal shards that catch the sun,
Each idea sparkling, never done.

Fragments merge in an elegant dance,
Creating patterns, a fleeting chance.
Through clarity, new visions rise,
The world transformed, a sweet surprise.

Moments freeze like dew on grass,
Captured whispers, as they pass.
In silent realms, innovations spark,
A radiant glow in the deepest dark.

In each reflection, wisdom gleams,
Unlocking pathways to hidden dreams.
Crystallized ideas, bright and bold,
A treasure trove of stories told.

Textured Truths

In layers deep, the truth resides,
Woven tales in woven tides.
Rough edges and soft, a complex weave,
In every stitch, a story to believe.

Life's tapestry, both dark and light,
Each thread a journey, a silent fight.
Rich in colors, textures collide,
Revealing facets that cannot hide.

Voices murmur through the years,
In every joy, in every fear.
Scarred pages tell of battles fought,
In textured truths, wisdom taught.

Through varied paths, we find our way,
In intricate patterns of night and day.
Embrace the layers, without disdain,
For in textured truths, we break the chain.

Lines That Bind

In whispers soft, our stories meet,
Threads of fate, woven complete.
From heart to heart, we find our way,
With every word, the shadows play.

Upon the canvas, colors blend,
Each stroke a truth, a hidden friend.
The ties we forge, though oft unseen,
Bind us close, in spaces between.

A tapestry of silent thought,
In every knot, a lesson taught.
Together we build, together we soar,
In the bond we share, forevermore.

In laughter shared, and tears we shed,
These lines we trace, where dreams are fed.
Through time and change, we dare to find,
The endless paths where love has signed.

Forming Connections

Across the miles, we reach and stretch,
In every glance, a bond we fetch.
The laughter shared, the secrets told,
In woven hearts, our truths unfold.

Moments linger, like morning dew,
In every beat, I sense you too.
A whisper here, a touch so light,
With every spark, we ignite the night.

In crowded rooms, you stand alone,
Yet in your smile, I've found a home.
It's in the silence, we both know,
The ties we form, they only grow.

With every encounter, we carve our space,
In shared glances, our dreams embrace.
Through every story, we subtly share,
In connections formed, our souls laid bare.

Rhythm in Relief

In the hush of night, we find our peace,
With every heartbeat, the world's release.
The gentle sway of time's embrace,
In silent moments, we find our place.

Rhythms echo in the calm of mind,
A soft reminder of what's aligned.
In breaths we take, release the fight,
Creating space for pure delight.

With every note, our worries fade,
In melodies of love, we're unafraid.
Chasing shadows, but not alone,
The rhythm guides us, love has grown.

In dawn's soft glow, we greet the day,
With every step, we find our way.
The rhythm flows, a stream so clear,
In relief, we dance, no need to fear.

The Floor Plan of Thought

In rooms of the mind, ideas collide,
With open doors, they cannot hide.
Blueprints drawn with the ink of dreams,
Through every crack, inspiration streams.

A hallway leads to questions profound,
Where echoes of wisdom wrap around.
In corners filled with shadows' embrace,
We find the light, we carve our space.

Windows of hope let the sun pour in,
In every glance, new journeys begin.
The laughter dances in open air,
In this design, our souls laid bare.

Together we build, from thought to form,
Through trials faced, we weather the storm.
In the floor plan of life, we lay our roots,
With every step, our spirit shoots.

Verse in Vividness

Colors swirl like dreams afloat,
In the canvas of the night.
Whispers of the past emoted,
In hues that burst with light.

A crimson dawn ignites the sky,
Golden rays in gentle dance.
Nature sings, oh, hear its cry,
As shadows take their chance.

Vivid creatures flit and play,
Beneath a sun so warm and bright.
They weave through branches, bright as day,
In this enchanting sight.

Heartbeats echo in the art,
Life pulsates in each heartbeat.
Every stroke, a brand-new start,
In color, we're complete.

Concrete Reality

Brick walls rise, unyielding gaze,
Paved roads in a resolute line.
Time ticks on through mundane days,
Each moment, a silent sign.

Workers toil beneath gray skies,
Their shadows cast long and lean.
Footsteps echo, the city sighs,
In the spaces in between.

The fountain's splash in midday light,
Children play by its cool stream.
Life unfolds in simple sight,
A dream within a dream.

Yet amidst the harsh and cold,
Hope shines bright in every heart.
In concrete's strength, stories told,
A world that won't depart.

Ethereal Shapes

Gossamer threads in twilight's fold,
Dancing softly, breezes sigh.
Whispers of the stories told,
In starlight's gentle eye.

Waves of mist like ghosts float by,
Caressing dreams that lie in wait.
Formless shadows brush the sky,
As night begins to gate.

Softly echoing through the night,
An unseen pulse, a beating heart.
Ethereal forms take playful flight,
In the dark, they're set apart.

Shapes of longing, soft and free,
In realms where silence falls like dew.
They shimmer with sweet mystery,
A dance for me and you.

Patterns in the Poem

Words align like stars in space,
Crafting tales that deeply flow.
In stanzas, we find our place,
A rhythm, soft and slow.

Lines entwine like lovers' hands,
Each verse a whisper in the dark.
In the silence, beauty stands,
Where echoes leave their mark.

Refrains linger like a song,
Inviting hearts to join the dance.
In the weave where we belong,
Each heartbeat finds a chance.

Patterns drawn in ink and fate,
In the poem, life unfolds.
With every line, a door, a gate,
A story waiting to be told.

Remnants of Reflection

In quiet pools, still waters lie,
Memories whisper, as clouds drift by.
Shadows dance on the surface clear,
Echoes of moments, we hold so dear.

Fragments of life, like leaves in fall,
Fleeting glances, we cannot recall.
In silence, we find what time forgets,
A tapestry woven with lost regrets.

Voices linger, soft and low,
In the heart's chamber, they ebb and flow.
Unraveled threads of a tangled past,
In hushed tones, their stories cast.

Reflection deep, in twilight's embrace,
Each ripple whispers, a tender trace.
Haunting the spaces where dreams abide,
In the depths of thought, we cannot hide.

Structure of Sentiment

Built on dreams, where feelings grow,
Each beam a promise, each wall a glow.
Foundations strong, yet fragile too,
In the heart's chambers, love breaks through.

Each window framed with hope and light,
Casting shadows, chasing night.
Vaulted ceilings of aspirations grand,
We paint our future with tender hands.

Bridges of trust, spanning the void,
Through storms and trials, never destroyed.
A sanctuary where tears can mend,
Crafted moments with time to spend.

Rooms resonate with laughter's sound,
A symphony of love unbound.
In this structure, we find our place,
A testament to the human race.

The Weight of Words

Carved in stone, or whispered low,
Words hold power, in ebb and flow.
They soar like birds, yet bind like chains,
A tender touch or bitter pains.

Pages turn with every thought,
In ink we bleed, in silence caught.
Softly spoken, they can ignite,
A fire within, bring forth the light.

With every syllable, breaths we share,
A tapestry woven with utmost care.
In the warmth of phrases, hearts can bloom,
But careless utterances can spell our doom.

Listen closely, in silence found,
The weight of words can shake the ground.
Crafted stories, we must embrace,
For in our speech, the truth we chase.

Poetic Architecture

Crafted verses like bricks align,
In a structure where starlight shines.
Each stanza stands, a sturdy frame,
Echoing whispers of love and pain.

Columns rise with rhythmic grace,
Holding dreams in an open space.
Arches curve like a lover's sigh,
Holding moments that never die.

Windows of light, with colors bright,
Reflecting passions in the night.
A sanctuary for thoughts to roam,
In every line, we find our home.

Rooftops kissed by the heavens high,
Sheltering hopes in the vast blue sky.
In this architecture, we construct,
A world where words forever conduct.

Textual Terrain

In the land of ink and dreams,
Words rise like ancient streams.
Fingertips trace the glyphs of old,
Stories wait, a treasure untold.

Mountains of prose, valleys of rhyme,
Echoes of laughter, whispers of time.
Each page a path, each line a way,
In this textual terrain, we play.

Winding through thoughts, lost and found,
Emotions dance, swirling around.
With every verse, a journey begins,
In the heart of the words, the adventure spins.

So we wander, curious and free,
In this vast landscape of poetry.
Where every line leads to a new view,
Navigating the realms, just me and you.

Patterns of the Heart

In the quiet of night, feelings collide,
Patterns emerge, where secrets reside.
Lines weave and thread in unison true,
Mapping the rhythm of me and you.

Like stars aligned in the velvet sky,
Whispers of love flutter and fly.
Each heartbeat echoes, a soft reprieve,
In this pattern, we endlessly weave.

Through joys and sorrows, a tapestry bright,
With threads of passion, we ignite the night.
Moments entwined, forever they stay,
In patterns of the heart, we find our way.

Let us dance in this intricate lace,
Embracing the chaos, finding our place.
Together we'll stitch the dreams from the start,
With every heartbeat, we create our art.

Wordscapes Unveiled

In the silence, whispers rise,
Crafting worlds beneath our skies.
Lost in realms where thoughts align,
Wordscapes unfold, divine and fine.

Each letter, a brush, colors we find,
Painting emotions, soft and unkind.
Illuminated paths where wanderers tread,
In the landscape of language, all fears shed.

Verse by verse, the story grows,
Hidden treasures in the prose.
As echoes linger, and shadows play,
Wordscapes unveil in a radiant display.

So let us wander, let us explore,
In the vast expanse, there's always more.
Together we'll navigate till the dawn,
In wordscapes unveiled, our souls reborn.

Fractured Syntax

In the chaos, meanings bend,
Fractured syntax, words transcend.
Thoughts collide like stars on high,
In this mess, the truth can fly.

Broken lines, a puzzle to solve,
As scattered pieces around us evolve.
With every pause, a breath we take,
In the fragments, new forms awake.

A sentence twists, a thought is spun,
In disarray, our hearts are won.
From discord, harmony may rise,
In fractured syntax, wisdom lies.

So embrace the splinters, the jumbled song,
For in the chaos, we all belong.
Let's find beauty where errors play,
In fractured syntax, we'll find our way.

Milton Keynes UK
Ingram Content Group UK Ltd.
UKHW020936041024
449263UK00011B/558

9 789916 881194